SHARK

Quarto is the authority on a wide range of topics.

Quarto educates, entertains and enriches the lives of
our readers—enthusiasts and lovers of hands-on living.

www.quartoknows.com

Design: Duck Egg Blue
Editor: Joanna McInerney

This library edition published in 2017 by Quarto Library.,
Part of The Quarto Group
6 Orchard, Lake Forest, CA 92630

Distributed in the United States and Canada by
Lerner Publisher Services
241 First Avenue North
Minneapolis, MN 55401 U.S.A.
www.lernerbooks.com

A CIP record for this book is available from the Library of Congress.

ISBN 978 1 68297 081 2

Printed in China

Contents

What is a shark?

Sharks are incredible fish. They are strong, silent animals that swim through the seas. Sharks are famous for their sharp teeth and deadly natures, but they are also beautiful ocean survivors that make our world a more interesting place.

Big fish

Most sharks are big fish, with long, slender bodies and tails. They hunt other animals to eat. Sharks swim through the ocean, chasing **shoals** of fish. All sharks use **gills** to breathe underwater.

That's amazing!

A shark's body is not covered in the smooth, colorful **scales** that other fish have. Their bodies are covered in rough, toothlike scales instead. They help sharks to swim fast.

Types of shark

There are two main types of shark. Larger sharks have big, powerful bodies and they usually swim fast, chasing food. Smaller sharks live near the **seabed** where they can hide among the rocks, coral, and **seaweed**. These sharks usually move slower than bigger sharks.

Meat eaters

All sharks are **predators**, which means they hunt for other animals to eat. Some sharks hunt big animals, such as baby whales or other sharks. Other sharks eat animals that are no bigger than a finger.

That's amazing!

Fast sharks are usually gray and white, brown, or blue-gray. Slow sharks are often patterned. This helps them to hide on the seabed. These patterns are called **camouflage**.

Hot and cold

Greenland sharks live in the icy waters near the **North Pole**. They swim slowly, because it is too cold for their muscles to move quickly. Reef sharks live in the warm shallow waters of a **coral reef**.

Where sharks live

Sharks live in seas and oceans all over the world in shallow and deep water. Bull sharks can survive in rivers. Sharks are most common in warm water, near the **coast**. Young sharks usually live close to land where there are more places to hide from predators.

That's amazing!

Great white sharks can live in almost any part of the ocean, but they prefer cool water. They often swim near the surface of the ocean, because this is where they find their **prey**.

9

Baby sharks

A baby shark is called a **pup**. Fast sharks give birth to their baby sharks. They usually have just a few pups at a time. Slow sharks that live near the seabed lay eggs instead of giving birth to pups. The pups **hatch** from the eggs.

Mermaid's purse

Horn sharks lay big eggs that are protected by a rubbery case, called a mermaid's purse. The mother does not look after her eggs, and they hatch about five months later.

That's amazing!

Baby sharks look after themselves. They swim away from their mother because she might get hungry and eat them! Pups can swim and hunt as soon as they are born, or hatch.

Slow movers

Basking sharks live in cooler water, and they grow to about 26 feet (8 m) long. They have long gill slits on the sides of their heads. They swim slowly with their mouths wide open.

That's amazing!

Whale sharks are the biggest fish in the world. They can grow to more than 39 feet (12 m) long. They live in warm seas where they slowly swim, looking for tiny shelled animals and fish eggs to eat.

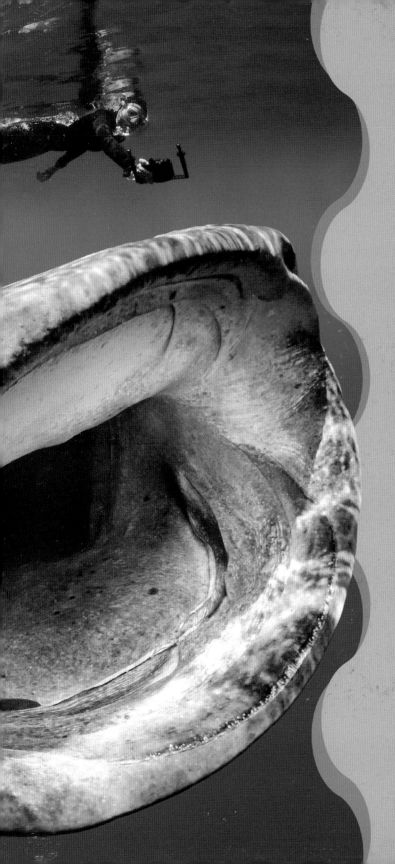

Big eaters

The biggest sharks do not chase fish to eat. Instead, they catch lots of tiny animals. These sharks take in mouthfuls of water that are full of little shrimp, baby fish, and other animals. The food is trapped in their mouths and the water passes out of their **gill slits**.

Hunters

Fast sharks are built for speed. When they smell, or see, their prey they chase it, grabbing it with their jaws. The fastest sharks in the world are called shortfin makos. Most sharks that live near the seabed are ambush hunters. This means they hide and then attack their prey by surprise.

Unfussy eaters

Hunting sharks are not fussy about what they eat. They hunt for other sharks, seals, fish, and **squid**. Some slow sharks have big, strong teeth that crunch through the hard skin of crabs and shelled sea animals.

That's amazing!

The size and shape of a shark's teeth are perfect for the type of food they prefer. Long, slender, and pointed teeth are good for gripping onto slippery fish and squid!

15

On the move

A shark's body is packed with muscles. It has fins on its back, its belly, and its sides. The fins stop a shark from rolling over in the water, and help it to turn left or right. Blue sharks are superb swimmers, and can go on journeys of 5,600 miles (9,000 km) or more!

Crawlers

Some slow sharks creep along the seabed. They use their fins like legs to crawl. As they move, they feel for food, such as shelled animals. Even "slow" sharks can swim and they move quickly when they need to.

That's amazing!

Hammerhead sharks have strange-shaped heads that are very wide. This shape helps them to change direction quickly. Their eyes are on the sides of their head, which means they can see well.

Staying safe

Not many ocean animals are big enough or strong enough to kill a shark. Baby sharks, however, are in more danger. While they are growing up they hide in coral reefs, near rocky **shores** where there are plenty of hiding places, or in seaweed.

Moving carpets

Wobbegongs are sharks that are camouflaged. They have flaps of skin that help them blend into the seabed. Their patterns and colors are so bold and beautiful that they are called carpet sharks!

That's amazing!

Swell sharks are shy. When they are scared they hide in a crack between rocks. They swallow air so they swell up, and nothing can pull them out of their hiding place!

Shark science

Biologists have helped us to understand how sharks live, but there is still plenty more to discover about these incredible creatures. Learning about sharks helps us to keep them safe for the future.

That's amazing!

Sharks want variety in their diets, just like humans. In an aquarium, a shark will refuse food if it has eaten the same thing too many times.

People and sharks

Many people are scared of sharks, but very few sharks are interested in humans. People are much more dangerous than sharks are. Millions of sharks are killed every year by people.

Glossary

Biologist

A person who finds out more about how animals and plants live is called a biologist.

Camouflage

When an animal's colors help it to hide, it is camouflaged.

Coast

The land that meets the sea is called a coast.

Coral reef

A coral reef is a rocky home to many animals under the sea. It is built by tiny animals called coral polyps.

Gills

Animals that breathe underwater have gills instead of lungs.

Gill slits

Openings where water flows out of a shark's gills.

Hatch
This is when an egg breaks open so the baby animal can get out.

North Pole
The place at the top of the world, where the winter is very long, cold, and dark, is called the North Pole.

Predator
An animal that hunts other animals is a predator.

Prey
An animal that is hunted by other animals is called prey.

Pup
A baby shark is called a pup.

Scales
Fish are covered in platelike scales. They are stronger than skin, and help protect the fish's body.

Seabed
This is the bottom of the sea or ocean. It is muddy, sandy, stony, or rocky.

Seaweed
Plants that live in the sea are called seaweed.

Shoal
A group of fish is called a shoal, or a school.

Shore
The shore is the place where the sea meets the land.

Squid
Squid are soft-bodied sea creatures with tentacles. They are similar to octopuses.

Index

Picture credits

(t=top, b=bottom, l=left, r=right, fc=front cover, bc=back cover)

Alamy

6bl Carlos Villoch - MagicSea.com, 6tr Greg Amptman, 8r Nature Picture Library, 12bl digitalunderwater.com, 14-15 Cultura Creative (RF), 16r Nature Picture Library, 16-17 Poelzer Wolfgang, 18bl Jeff Rotman, 18t WaterFrame, 20-21 Westend61 GmbH,

Nature Picture Library

7r Visuals Unlimited, 16r Brandon Cole

Seapics

4-5 Reinhard Dirscherl, 10br Howard Hall, 10bl, 12-13 Andy Murch, 13br Tom Haight, 14bl Masa Ushioda, 18-19 David Wrobel, 19r Hideyuki Utsunomiya,

Shutterstock

1t Sphinx Wang, 1b, 5tr, 6-7 frantisekhojdysz, 2-3 Evdokimov Maxim, 4bl tubuceo, 4tr Ian Scott, 8b Andrea Izzotti, 8-9 Andrey Armyagov, 9br Jose Angel Astor Rocha, 10-11 © Marleenwolters, 11br conceptfoto.ru, 14r, 17tr Martin P, 15b MP cz, 16bl Joost van Uffelen, 20tr Greg Amptman, 21br Durden Images